I0418395

You Want Me to Do WHAT
A Caregiver's Guide to Losing Your Sanity

Judith Bennett

You Want Me to Do WHAT Now?
A Caregiver's Guide to Losing Your Sanity
© Judith Bennett Media, 2025

All rights reserved. No part of this book may be reproduced, stored in a retrieval system, or transmitted in any form or by any means — electronic, mechanical, photocopying, recording, or otherwise — without the prior written permission of the author, except for brief quotes used in reviews or articles.

This book is a work of nonfiction. Some names and identifying details have been changed to protect the privacy of individuals.

This book has been self-published.
Printed in the United States of America

ISBN: 9798998543807

For permissions or inquiries, contact:

JudithBennettMedia@gmail.com

Cover art created using AI image generators

Dedicated to all my Angels.

For every caregiver who has ever laughed through exhaustion, cried in hospital parking lots, or kept going when they thought they couldn't—
This is for you.

To love someone deeply is to show up — again and again, even when it's hard, even when you're exhausted, even when they don't realize you're the reason they're still standing.

Contents

Preface

I never planned on becoming a caregiver. No one handed me an application, no recruiter sat me down for an interview, and there certainly wasn't a training manual. One day, I was just… doing it. And once I started, I didn't stop.

For thirty years, my life revolved around taking care of others — my father, my grandmother, my fiancé, and, finally, my mother. I managed doctor's appointments, hospital stays, insurance battles, medication schedules, and an ever-growing pile of stress. Somewhere along the way, I became fluent in medical jargon, mastered the art of eating cold meals standing up, and accepted that my "free time" was about as real as a unicorn.

This book is not your typical caregiving memoir. Yes, it's about the hard stuff — the exhaustion, the heartbreak, the moments when you feel like you have nothing left to give. But it's also about the funny stuff — the absurd moments, the coping mechanisms, the times I found myself thinking, *Seriously? This is my life?* Because if there's one thing I've learned, it's that you **have to laugh** — even in the face of total chaos.

If you're a caregiver, you'll recognize yourself in these pages. If you've ever loved someone through sickness, you'll understand the highs and lows. And if you're here just for the entertainment value — buckle up, because this ride is anything but smooth.

1

This is my story. The good, the bad, the hilarious, and the downright WTF moments of caregiving.

So, grab a cup of coffee (or something stronger), settle in, and let's get through this together.

Because if you've ever found yourself saying, **"You want me to do WHAT now?"** — welcome to the club.

Chapter One: Welcome to the Caregiver Circus

"They never tell you that caregiving is basically signing up for a full-time job with no training, no sleep, and a boss who may or may not throw things at you. Oh, and the pay? Nonexistent. Welcome to the circus."

I didn't apply for this job. There was no orientation, no handbook, and certainly no fancy HR department to complain to when things got insane. One day, I was just living my life—working, attempting to have a social life, and pretending to be a fully functioning adult. The next thing I knew, I was juggling doctor's appointments, medications, late-night panic attacks, and an ever-growing pile of laundry.

People love to romanticize caregiving. They throw around phrases like, *"It's such an honor to take care of a loved one,"* and *"You're so strong."* And sure, there were moments of deep love and connection. But there were also moments of pure, unfiltered chaos. Like when my mother decided she didn't need to listen to her doctor anymore, or when my fiancé flat-out refused to take his cancer treatments because he *felt fine.*

Caregiving is a mix of love, exhaustion, dark humor, and an occasional urge to run away to a deserted island. This is my story. It's messy, it's ridiculous, and, somehow, it's also one of the most meaningful things I've ever done.

Meet the Cast of My Caregiving Chaos

If you're going to survive the caregiving world, you need a sense of humor and a strong stomach. And if you're reading this book, you're either a caregiver yourself (in which case, I salute you), or you just really enjoy reading about other people's suffering. Either way, welcome!

Before we go any further, let's introduce the key players in my wild production.

⚜ My Mother – The Stubborn Queen

- Fiercely independent, opinionated, and not afraid to ignore doctor's orders if they didn't suit her mood.
- Loved me endlessly but also loved arguing with me for sport.

☺ My Father – The Old-School Gentleman

- Much older than my mother, which meant I spent most of my childhood mentally preparing for his death (spoiler: all that preparation did NOT help).
- Had a quiet strength but also an unmatched talent for pretending not to hear my mother's complaints.

☠ My Former Fiancé – The Most Stubborn Cancer Patient in History

- The king of procrastination, especially when it came to medical treatment.
- Once decided he was *"cured"* halfway through chemo and just… stopped going.

😇 Me – The One Who Didn't Know What She Signed Up For

- Thought she was going to have a normal adulthood but instead became a full-time caregiver, human crisis manager, and unpaid medical assistant.
- Developed a strong "smile through the madness" approach to life.
- Once Googled "can stress actually kill you?" at 3 a.m.

Now that you've met the main characters, let's dive into how I ended up here.

Chapter Two: The People Who Made Me

If you had asked me as a kid what I wanted to be when I grew up, I would have said something normal — a teacher, a veterinarian, maybe even an astronaut if I was feeling ambitious.

At no point did I ever say, *"I'd like to become a full-time caregiver before I even hit 30."*

Yet, here we are.

Of course, looking back, there were warning signs that my life would be a little different. Let's start with my parents.

Growing Up with an Older Dad

My dad was 55 when I was born. While most of my friends had young, energetic fathers who played catch and fixed things around the house, my dad was more like a history professor who occasionally napped in his recliner. Despite his age, my father did all the things the young, energetic fathers did, but, best of all, my father did his best to provide me with the wisdom I would need for the future.

Due to my father's age, and my juvenile thinking, I was convinced that any day now he was going to drop dead.

At five years old, I remember thinking, *"If Dad dies, what do we do?"*

At ten, I upgraded my plan: *"If Dad dies, I'll make sure Mom is okay."*

At fifteen, I added a new detail: *"If Dad dies, I'll make sure Mom is okay, and I'll be the strong one."*

Spoiler alert: All that mental preparation did nothing.

My Mother: The Queen of Stubbornness

My mother was 35 when she had me. She was loving, fiercely independent, and had a master's degree in giving unsolicited advice.

Growing up, she often referred to me as "the project." I was her and my father's project. She wasn't a super strict mother, but she thrived on setting a consistent home life for me growing up.

Something about my mother. She never admitted when she needed help.

If you offered to carry groceries: *"No, I got it."*
If you suggested she go to the doctor: *"It's nothing, I'll be fine."*
If you pointed out she was clearly limping: *"I'm not limping, I'm walking with character."*

As you can see, caregiving for her was going to be a challenge.

7

The Great Musical Instrument Debate

My parents loved watching television shows that featured big band music. Growing up, that is where my love of music started. I can remember sitting on the floor, watching the television, which was a fairly small screen nestled in a large wood cabinet. Flat screens have NOTHING on the old television sets that were truly furniture pieces.

When I was in 5th grade, I changed elementary schools. I was now in a school that had a band. I was so excited, I remember coming home from the first day of school, telling my parents there was a school band and I wanted to be in it. I remember them asking me what instrument I wanted to play, and I eagerly said the trumpet!

At first, I thought the trumpet would be a great choice. Three keys? How hard could it be?

My father, a self-taught music expert, sat me down and patiently explained that while the trumpet *looked* easy, it was actually very hard to play. He told me it would leave me with a very sore mouth, lips that would be swollen, and cheeks that would expand to three times the normal size.

Fine. Whatever. I moved on.

One day, I heard "The Entertainer" by Scott Joplin on TV. It had a clarinet solo, and I thought, *That's it. That's my instrument.*

Thus began my clarinet journey, which included:
✓ Private lessons (because both my parents were committed to this)
✓ Daily practice sessions (which my father supervised like a drill sergeant)
✓ An expensive investment in a $2,000 Buffet clarinet from France

My clarinet and I had a love-hate relationship.

There were days when I wanted to quit. Practicing was hard. But my dad never let me give up.

He was there every night after dinner, helping me with finger placements, encouraging me when I got frustrated, and reminding me that I could do anything. As I look back on it now, he never got to enjoy his after-dinner coffee because he was always helping me practice.

His dedication paid off. I made it into All-County and All-State music competitions and even received a partial music scholarship for college.

But don't get too excited — because in true ironic fashion, I didn't pursue music in college.

Marching Band, Potholes, and Public Embarrassment

My musical career may not have lasted, but it did earn me the title of Drum Majorette my senior year of high school.

You Want Me to Do WHAT Now? - Judith Bennett

This meant I got to lead the band in our town's Memorial Day parade.

A parade, I should mention, that required me to march backward while conducting the band.

I bet you see where this is going.

There I was, in front of the town library, spectators cheering, flags waving, my big moment.

And then it happened.

I didn't see the pothole.

I tripped.

I fell.

I rolled slightly.

But—I never lost the beat.

The band? They kept playing, like the band on the sinking Titanic.

The trombone section, however, was very concerned.

One of them yelled:

"Oh my God, is she dead?!"

No, buddy, just my dignity.

By the time we reached the end of the parade, my parents were there waiting. The expression on my face gave away my mood. There was no hiding my current state of mind.

"Did the band not listen to you?" my mom asked.

I sighed.

"No, they listened. I just decided to fall down and go boom in front of thousands of people."

Off to the hospital we went.

Diagnosis? A sprained ankle.

Lesson?

Sometimes life knocks you down.

And when it does, you get back up, keep going, and pretend like nothing happened.

The First Signs of Caregiving

Looking back, my caregiving journey started long before I realized it.

My dad was slowing down, and my mother was refusing to admit when she needed help. Without thinking twice, I stepped in to assist.

It was small things at first. Carrying the groceries. Running errands. Attending doctor's appointments.

You Want Me to Do WHAT Now? - Judith Bennett

Until one day, I woke up and realized:

I was no longer just a daughter.

I was becoming a caregiver.

Chapter Three: Caregiving, Ready or Not

You don't wake up one day and say, *"You know what? I think I'd like to become a full-time caregiver."*

Nope. It sneaks up on you.

One day, you're just helping out — grabbing groceries, driving to doctor's appointments, making the occasional phone call.

And then suddenly, BOOM!

You're managing medications, insurance battles, meal planning, emotional meltdowns, and playing the role of part-time detective (because someone, somewhere, is definitely hiding something from you).

Caregiving doesn't give you a heads-up.

It doesn't ease you in with a training period.

It just drops you into the deep end and expects you to swim.

Why Me? Because My Mother Was Already on Duty

My caregiving journey began at the ripe age of 18, just shy of my 19th birthday. I was in college, just starting my adult life. As my father started to decline, my mother was already stretched thin.

She was splitting her time between caring for him and helping my grandmother.

My grandmother was fiercely independent (read: stubborn), but as she aged, she needed more help — help that my mother took on without hesitation.

So, while she was busy managing her mother's needs, the bulk of my father's care fell to me.

I wasn't just helping; I was stepping into a full-time role before I even realized it.

And once I was in, there was no getting out.

The Day My Father Stopped Driving

If there was one moment that made me realize my dad was really aging, it was the day he gave up his car keys.

My father was a man of routine.

He had his favorite diners, grocery stores, and doctors, and he liked being in control of his own transportation.

But as his health declined, things started getting dangerous. His reflexes weren't what they used to be and his vision was getting more and more limited due to cataracts.

It was time.

The day he officially stopped driving; I thought it would be emotional.

Instead, he just handed me the keys, sighed, and said, *"Well, I guess you're my chauffeur now."*

And just like that, at age 22, I became his personal driver—unpaid, and with far more backseat driving critiques.

Balancing Caregiving and Dating

Somehow, in the middle of all this, I was dating and had met the man who would eventually become my fiancé.

He was supportive of everything I had going on, but let's be honest, dating me was not easy.

Between juggling my job, my father's increasing needs, and my mother being busy with my grandmother, I had very little free time.

Date night had to be planned strategically—usually sandwiched between doctor's appointments and grocery store runs.

I would leave work, pick up whatever my dad needed, drop it off, check on him, and then sprint out the door to make it to dinner.

If my boyfriend was wondering what dating me would be like long-term, he was getting a crash course real fast.

Steroids, Snacks, and Puffy Lung

A "puffy lung" is what doctors called my father's condition. I had never heard of this in my life. It sounded like something a cartoon character would get. But what it **actually** meant was:

✓ The doctors had no real answers.
✓ He was about to be put on a six-month steroid treatment.

The steroids helped his breathing, but with one very unexpected side effect:

>His appetite turned into a monster.

>I mean a full-blown, never-satisfied, 24/7 eating machine.

One day, I came home to find my father sitting in his chair, surrounded by empty snack wrappers.

Me: *Dad… what happened?*
Dad: *I don't know, I got hungry.*

He had eaten EVERYTHING.

A lifetime supply of Mallomars? Gone.
An entire loaf of bread? Toasted and devoured.

Leftovers that were supposed to last the week? Vanished without a trace.

This was not normal.

Turns out, steroids make you hungry. And when you're already a man who enjoys a good meal? It's a disaster waiting to happen.

The next time I went to the grocery store, I hid the snacks like we were in the middle of a zombie apocalypse.

That only led to more problems.

Dad: *Where's the food?*
Me: *What food?*
Dad: *You think you're funny?*
Me: *A little.*

Steroid Dad was no joke. All this overeating led to another diagnosis, Steroid Induced Type 2 Diabetes. Sure, why not?!

Survival Mode Kicks In

At this point, I was juggling:

✔ Working full-time
✔ Driving my dad everywhere
✔ Managing his medications
✔ Keeping track of his endless medical

appointments
✓ Trying to maintain a relationship and some sense of normalcy

◼ **Survival Mode Symptoms Include:**
✓ Sleeping with one eye open
✓ Knowing every doctor's office hold music by heart
✓ Developing the patience of a saint (or completely losing it — no in-between)
✓ Showing up to dates exhausted but pretending to be fine

I wasn't giving up my relationship, but I also wasn't able to be fully present in it.

And I knew it.

It was hard.

I wanted to be in love, be carefree, and have the kind of dating experience other people had.

Instead, I was rushing from crisis to crisis, hoping I wasn't neglecting anyone.

Chapter Four: When Life Says "Plot Twist"

Caregiving is a lot like being in an escape room, except there's no way out, and the room keeps catching on fire.

Just when you think you've got things under control, something happens that completely throws you off balance.

In my case?

That *something* was my father's stroke.

And just to make things more *fun*, it happened on a day already filled with stress and emotions.

September 11, 2002: A Stroke, Because Why Not?

It was September 11, 2002. Yes, THAT September 11. It was the one-year anniversary of the terrorist attacks.

My parents had planned to go to the Bronx Zoo that day, but at the last minute, they changed their minds and stayed home.

Instead, they were watching the memorial services on TV when it happened.

One minute, my father was sitting in his recliner.

The next, he lifted both arms into the air like he was trying to grab something.

My mother, alarmed, asked, *"What are you doing?"*

His response?

"I fell."

Except… he was still sitting in his chair.

My mother immediately called 911, then called me.

I was at work.

I dropped everything and met them at the hospital.

After hours of scans and tests, the doctors confirmed it: he had suffered a stroke.

And here's the fun part—the next few days were critical because his brain could swell. If that happened, they might have to perform surgery to relieve the pressure. I remember meeting with the surgeon, who said that if the pressure got bad enough, she was going to have to drill a hole in his skull to relieve that pressure. Thinking of it now, of having someone drill a hole into your skull, was a very scary possibility.

Thankfully, surgery wasn't necessary.

But the stroke left him with limited use of his arm and leg on his left side.

Rehab: Where Dad Had Zero Patience

This meant he needed physical therapy.

So, off to rehab he went.

You'd think rehab would be a place of progress and motivation—where patients, encouraged by hopeful therapists, push themselves to regain their independence.

For my father?

It was a place of irritation, it was a place full of strangers, it wasn't home.

The physical therapists meant well. They were patient. They were encouraging. They tried so hard to get him moving. But the stroke affected his mental well-being even more than his physical limitations.

Negotiations (or, My Failed Attempts at Bribery)

My mother and I tried everything to motivate him:
✔ **Logic:** *Dad, you have to do this if you want to come home.*
✔ **Guilt:** *Mom is exhausted, you need to get stronger to help her.*
✔ **Bribery:** *If you do your therapy today, I'll bring you Nathan's hot dogs.*

His response?

✓ A grumble.
✓ A wave of his hand.
✓ A classic dad eye-roll.

It was like arguing with a brick wall—except the brick wall would at least pretend to listen.

Giving Up Before the Fight Even Started

The hardest part?

I think, deep down, he already knew he wasn't coming home.

He had spent his whole life being independent—the strong provider, the head of the family.

And now, he couldn't stand up on his own.

He couldn't walk without help.

He couldn't even control the things that were happening to his own body.

I think a part of him decided—what's the point?

And honestly?

That made it even harder to push him.

Because how do you tell someone to fight when they're already convinced they've lost?

The Final ER Visit

The rehab facility lasted just over a week before things took a turn for the worse.

One night, my mother got a call from the facility:

"Your husband has developed an infection, and we're sending him to the ER."

Infection?

Oh.

Sepsis.

And just like that, he was back in the hospital.

This time, for the last time.

"Don't Kick the Can" — The Moment He Let Go

By the time my mother and I arrived at the hospital, my father was hooked up to lots of machines, and IV antibiotics. He had just come back from radiology where they checked to see if he had suffered another stroke, which he hadn't. I remember my father trying to speak to me with his oxygen mask on, which was large and covered his mouth. I could hear him, but he wasn't making sense. So I just stood there, smiling at him and nodding my head yes. After some time, my father closed his eyes and fell asleep.

My mother and I sat by his hospital bed, watching his breathing slow down.

At one point, we decided to take a quick break and step outside for air.

As we walked away from his bed, my mother accidentally kicked a trash can. I, in my exhausted, grief-laced sarcasm, said:

"Mom, don't kick the can."

At that *exact moment*, I was suddenly overcome with an intense warmth.

It wasn't just a temperature change — it was a feeling.

A deep, overwhelming sense of love.

We didn't know it yet, but that was the moment my father passed.

The Aftermath: No Time to Grieve (Because Grief Doesn't Come with a Pause Button)

When you lose someone, you expect life to pause.

Just for a second.

Just long enough to catch your breath.

But life?

It doesn't pause for anything.

It just keeps going.

Grief on a Time Crunch

My father had just passed away. I was 27 years old, too young to have lost my father.

My mother had just lost her husband.

And yet, there was no time to sit with the loss.

No time to break down.

No time to process.

Because while we were both grieving, we had someone else to worry about.

My grandmother.

A New Level of Exhaustion

She had loved my father dearly.

She was devastated.

But she was also in her 80s, with mobility issues and growing health concerns.

Which meant?

She now needed even more care than before. My mother, fresh in her own grief, had to shift immediately into caregiver mode. I had to step up even more, supporting both my mother and my grandmother. The weight of loss was sitting on our shoulders, but there was no time to address it.

It was like drowning in sadness but still having to swim — because someone else was holding onto you, needing to stay afloat.

Chapter Five: Ignoring Fred

If there was a moment in life where I thought, *you've got to be kidding me*, it was this one. Several years had passed since my father died. During those years, my career had really taken off, and I was considered "senior" in my profession.

I was still helping my mother and grandmother, working hard to balance both of them as well as my fiancé, and trying to figure out life.

And then, because life apparently thought I wasn't busy enough, my fiancé decided it was his turn to join the Sick Person Club.

I mean, sure. Why not? I was 33 years old, how much harder could my life get? That was the understatement of the year.

A Cough That Wouldn't Quit

It started as a cold.

A simple, annoying, *no-big-deal* head cold.

✓ Stuffy nose
✓ Sore throat
✓ Cough

The first two symptoms disappeared after about a week.

The cough didn't.

At first, we thought it was just lingering. No big deal. Happens all the time.

Me: *Maybe you should go to the doctor?*
Fiancé: *I'm fine.*
Me: *Are you though?*
Fiancé: *Yes.*

He was not, in fact, fine.

After weeks of nagging, he finally caved and went to the doctor.

The doctor prescribed a steroid—the same one my father had been on for his "puffy lung." It was only a one-week treatment, and surprisingly, the cough got better.

We both thought, *Great! Problem solved!* Until the steroid treatment ended. The cough came right back. So back to the doctor he went.

This time, the doctor wasn't playing around.

✓ **Chest X-ray**
✓ **CT scan**
✓ **MRI**
✓ **Ultrasound**
✓ **Biopsy**

It was the biopsy that told us everything.

Meet Fred: The Uninvited Guest

"It's Hodgkin's Lymphoma."

I remember hearing those words and trying not to cry. I failed. The oncologist handed me a box of tissues while my fiancé sat there, completely stoic.

The doctor went on to explain that Hodgkin's Lymphoma had a high survival rate, and that because the tumor was small (about the size of a quarter), six months of chemotherapy should take care of it.

As my brain was trying to wrap itself around the diagnosis that would totally change both of our lives, I blurted out a name.

"Fred."

Fiancé: *...What?*

Me: *The tumor. It's Fred. We don't like Fred.*

He stared at me like I had lost my mind. Which, to be fair, maybe I had. But in my defense, I needed to find a way to make this easier to process. Giving the tumor a name made it feel less scary and more like an enemy we could fight. I'm honestly not sure why I blurted out "Fred," it's not like I had an arch enemy named Fred. It's just a name that popped into my head.

My fiancé liked the idea.

From that moment on, we didn't talk about *cancer*.

29

We talked about Fred.

Fred was an uninvited guest, a "squatter" who needed to be evicted.

And we were going to make sure he got kicked out.

Fred's Eviction Plan: Chemo, Round One

The standard treatment for Hodgkin's Lymphoma is a combination of four different chemo drugs:

- Adriamycin
- Bleomycin Sulfate
- Vinblastine Sulfate
- Dacarbazine

(Or ABVD, if you want to sound fancy.)

Together, these drugs attack cancer cells by stopping them from dividing and growing. Each infusion took about three hours. Twelve infusions over six months.

The plan was simple.

✔ Go to chemo.
✔ Kill Fred.
✔ Survive.

Except, there was one problem.

My fiancé absolutely hated doctors.

And hospitals.

And needles.

And literally everything involved with treating cancer.

The Port Fight of 2008

The oncologist wanted to surgically insert a port in my fiancé's chest. Ports make chemo easier, because instead of sticking a new vein every time, they can use the port for all the IVs, meds, and blood draws.

Seems logical, right?

Not to my fiancé.

Him: *Nope. Not happening.*
Me: *It will make this whole thing easier.*
Him: *I don't care.*

I argued. I begged. I bribed.

Nothing worked.

So instead of a chest port, we had to find an oncologist willing to use a PICC line — which is basically a long IV inserted into the upper arm.

That, he was fine with.

I'll never understand his logic.

But hey — at least we were finally starting chemo.

The First Chemo Treatment

I could tell he was scared, but he refused to admit it.

And he absolutely refused to take any kind of anti-anxiety medication.

So, instead of being calm and relaxed for his first infusion, he was a ball of nerves.

✓ Tapping his foot
✓ Clenching his jaw
✓ Acting like he might bolt at any second

I half-expected him to rip out the IV and make a run for it.

But somehow, he made it through.

Surprisingly?

The first treatment wasn't that bad. He had mild nausea but no vomiting. He was a little tired, but nothing extreme. I thought, *hey, maybe this won't be as bad as we expected!*

The oncologist had warned us, though:

"The side effects will get worse over time."

You Want Me to Do WHAT Now? - Judith Bennett

And wow, was that an understatement.

Chapter Six: When Fred Throws a Tantrum

Ah, the halfway mark of chemo.

A milestone!

A turning point!

A critical moment in the battle against Fred!

… Unless you're my fiancé.

Then, apparently, it's the perfect time to call it quits.

The Mid-Treatment Check-In

By the time we reached the sixth chemo treatment, things were going well. Fred was shrinking, the cough was totally gone. So, naturally, my fiancé's brain processed this as:

"Well, clearly, I don't need chemo anymore!"

Me: *… That is not how this works.*
Fiancé: *But I feel fine!*
Me: *Yes, because the chemo is WORKING.*

Him: *Nope. I'm done. I'm not going back.*

This was a very, very bad decision.

Cancelling Chemo Appointments Like They Were Brunch Plans

I will never understand the level of confidence this man had in his ability to self-diagnose. He had no medical degree. No formal training. No X-ray vision.

All he had was a gut feeling that he was cured after six chemo sessions instead of twelve.

And so, without hesitation, he called the oncology office and cancelled all remaining treatments.

✔ Treatment #7? Cancelled.
✔ Treatment #8? Nope.
✔ Treatment #9 through #12? Who needs 'em?

The oncology team was NOT happy.

They tried everything to convince him to come back.

✘ Logic? Didn't work.
✘ Scare tactics? Didn't work.
✘ Bribery? I tried. (Video games, new computer, even a dream car. NOTHING.)

He was done.

And that was the beginning of the end—for both his health and our relationship.

Cracks in the Foundation

At first, I tried to let it go.

I tried to tell myself:

✓ *If he was still sick, he would feel it.*
✓ *If Fred was still around, he would cough again.*
✓ *If cancer was still in his body, it would do… something.*

And for a while, my fiancé seemed fine.

He was eating normally.
He was gaining some weight back.
He was going to work.

But deep down?

I knew something had shifted. And not just with his health — with us. I had spent months fighting for him. Dragging him to chemo. Taking care of him when he felt like crap. Doing everything I could to make sure he survived this.

And he just threw it all away.

Resentment, Party of One

I was angry.

✓ Angry that he ignored medical advice.
✓ Angry that he didn't care enough to finish treatment.
✓ Angry that I had given so much and he just… quit.

That anger didn't go away.

It started seeping into everything. I stopped trying as hard. I stopped caring about his excuses. I stopped feeling like his partner and more like his annoyed roommate. I had fought for him harder than he had fought for himself.

And that realization?

It broke something between us.

Living in Two Different Realities

For him, life was back to normal.

✓ No more chemo.
✓ No more hospital visits.
✓ No more thinking about cancer.

For me?

✓ I was still waiting for the other shoe to drop.
✓ I was still waiting for Fred to come back.
✓ I was still waiting for him to admit that maybe, just maybe, he had made a mistake.

But he never did.

Instead, he **doubled down.**

✓ *"I told you I was fine."*
✓ *"You worry too much."*
✓ *"Stop treating me like I'm sick."*

So I did.

I stopped bringing it up.

I stopped nagging him about doctors.

And I let him live in his fantasy.

Because I was too exhausted to keep fighting a battle he refused to acknowledge.

Rebuilding a "Normal" Life

With cancer *"behind us"* (HA), we tried to move forward.

✓ I joined a gym.
✓ I focused on my career.
✓ I tried to find happiness again.

But under the surface? I was still holding onto that anger. I resented how selfish he had been. I resented how dismissive he was of everything I had done for him.

And honestly?

I started resenting him.

Two Years of Pretending

This cycle of denial, resentment, and pretending everything was fine lasted two years. Two years of ignoring Fred. Two years of waiting for the inevitable. Two years of feeling trapped in a relationship that no longer felt like a partnership. I was now 35 years old, how much more time was I going to put into this waiting game?

And then?

Fred came back.

Bigger. Stronger. And PISSED.

Because you can't just ghost cancer.

And this time?

Fred wasn't playing around.

Chapter Seven: Fred Comes Back Swinging

You know what's funny about cancer? It doesn't care if you're "done" with it. It doesn't care if you've decided, *"Nah, I don't feel like doing chemo anymore."* It doesn't care if you've spent two years pretending it doesn't exist.

Cancer is a petty little bastard.

And Fred?

Fred was about to make sure we knew it.

The Warning Signs

For a while, things seemed fine.

Or, at least, fine enough. He wasn't coughing. He wasn't losing weight. He wasn't showing obvious signs of being sick.

But then little things started creeping in. His energy wasn't the same. He started losing weight—slowly, but noticeably. He started complaining about pain in his chest.

Me: *Maybe you should go to the doctor?*
Him: *I'm fine.*

Me: *Are you though?*
Him: *Yes.*

He was not, in fact, fine.

Denial, Part Two

At this point, I was exhausted. I had spent years fighting for him. I had spent years watching him ignore reality. And now, I was watching it all happen — again.

And honestly?

I didn't have it in me to fight him anymore.

So, I just... stopped trying.

Me: *Okay.*

And that was it.

No more pushing. No more nagging.

Just silence.

Because I knew what was coming.

And when it finally hit him?

I was going to let him be the one to panic.

The Moment Reality Hit

It happened out of nowhere. We were watching TV, and he laughed.

And suddenly —

The cough was back.

He froze.

I froze.

We both knew exactly what that meant.

But instead of saying anything, we just… kept watching TV.

✓ Pretending we didn't hear it.
✓ Pretending it wasn't happening.
✓ Pretending Fred hadn't just announced his return.

But Fred didn't care about our little game.

Because the next day, the cough was worse.

And the day after that?

It was worse again.

And by the end of the week?

He was coughing constantly.

Fred's Comeback Tour: Bigger & Worse Than Ever

He finally caved and went to the doctor.

They ran all the same tests as before.

✔ Chest X-ray
✔ CT scan
✔ MRI
✔ Biopsy

And then, the doctor called us in. I had seen this movie before. I knew what was coming. But this time? The news was so much worse.

Fred Had a Party. And We Weren't Invited.

The tumor that was once the size of a quarter?

✔ It had quadrupled in size.
✔ It was now pressing against his right lung and heart.
✔ It was growing INTO his chest cavity.
✔ It had eaten through the bone, creating an actual hole in his chest, about the size of a silver dollar. The hole literally appeared overnight. It started out looking like an indentation, and when my fiancé touched it, the skin disintegrated and there was a hole.

Me: *Oh my god.*
Doctor: *Yeah.*

43

Apparently, when you ghost cancer, it doesn't just sit around waiting for an apology. It grows. Aggressively. And now, Fred was huge. And pissed.

And ready to finish what he started.

The New Plan: If You Want to Live, You Have to Actually Try

The oncologist did not hold back.

Doctor: *We don't have the luxury of taking our time anymore.*
Doctor: *This tumor is more advanced than before.*
Doctor: *This time, it won't respond to regular chemo alone.*

My fiancé just sat there, completely silent.

Because for the first time since his diagnosis, he wasn't in denial of just how sick he truly was.

And as much as I wanted to say, *"I told you so,"* I didn't.

Because what was the point?

We were out of time for stubbornness.

And for once?

He knew it.

Chapter Eight: Evicting Fred, Part Two

The first time **Fred** showed up, my fiancé treated cancer like a minor inconvenience.

Like it was some annoying telemarketer calling at dinner—just something to be ignored until it eventually went away.

✔ He ignored doctors. *They're probably overreacting.*
✔ He skipped chemo. *Who needs all twelve treatments when I feel fine after six?*
✔ He pretended it wasn't happening. *Denial is a legitimate strategy, right?*

And for a while?

That worked.

Until it didn't.

This Time? Fred Came to Win.

Fast forward two years.

Fred had evolved.

Fred had multiplied.

Fred had decided that just growing wasn't enough — he wanted to make an exit through my fiancé's chest.

Because it turns out, when you can **physically see** your cancer every time you take your shirt off...

It gets a little harder to pretend it's not there.

Fred, Now in 3D

I remember the first time I saw the hole.

It was about the size of a silver dollar.

Not just a wound.

A gaping, open space where tissue should have been.

And when I looked inside?

I could literally see his body cavity.

It was one of those moments where your brain struggles to catch up with reality.

The New Treatment Plan

The oncologist wasn't sugarcoating anything.

Doctor: *We're past the easy options.*
Doctor: *You'll need stronger chemo, a stem cell transplant,*

and radiation.
Doctor: *And this time, you have to finish it.*

And for the first time ever, my fiancé didn't argue.

He just nodded.

Because he finally got it.

The Chemo (Round Two, No Quitting Allowed)

This time, the chemo was stronger.

✓ New drugs.
✓ More side effects.
✓ Way more appointments.

But shockingly — my fiancé actually handled it well.

Why?

Because he finally agreed to take anti-anxiety medication.

The same meds he refused last time.

✓ No more fighting me every chemo day.
✓ No more panic attacks in the parking lot.
✓ No more trying to bribe him to go.

Instead, he walked in, sat down, and took the damn chemo.

And honestly?

I didn't know whether to be relieved or furious that we could've had it this easy the first time around.

The Staph Infection That Almost Ended It All

Then, because nothing could ever be easy, my fiancé developed a staph infection in his newly implanted PICC line.

Which meant:

✓ The PICC line had to come out and be inserted in his other arm.
✓ He needed a month of IV antibiotics.
✓ His chemo got delayed.

I had to administer the IV meds at home every single day.

By this point, I was basically a nurse:

✓ Chemo scheduler.
✓ IV antibiotic administrator.
✓ PICC line supervisor.
✓ Full-time worrier.

I was running on adrenaline and rage.

Oh, and I was still working a full-time job as a paralegal!

And we weren't even at the hardest part yet.

The Stem Cell Transplant Prep: The Injection Incident

Before the transplant, he had to take medication that would help his stem cells get harvested.

The process?

✔ Get a special injection the night before.
✔ The injection would tell his bone marrow to release thousands of stem cells.
✔ The next day, his blood would be filtered through a machine to collect them.

Sounds simple, right?

Except for one problem.

He refused to let me give him the shot.

Him: *I'll be fine without it.*
Me: *No, you won't.*

Him: *They won't even know.*
Me: *Oh, they'll know.*

And sure enough —

The next day, they hooked him up to the machine... and barely any stem cells came out.

Doctor: *Did you take the injection?*

Him: *… Yes.*
Doctor: *Are you sure?*
Him: *… Okay, no.*

I wanted to scream.

So we had to reschedule everything.

The next night, he allowed me to give him the shot, and the harvesting of his stem cells was a success.

Imagine that.

Chapter Nine: The Transplant That Changed Everything

By this point, I had done everything I could for him. I had fought for him when he wouldn't fight for himself. I had dragged him to appointments he didn't want to go to. I had argued with insurance companies and doctors. I had quite literally injected him with medication so he wouldn't screw up his own treatment.

And now?

Now we were at the final battle.

The stem cell transplant.

The Process: Wiping Him Out to Save Him

The stem cell transplant process was essentially this:

1. Kill off every last cancer cell.
2. Destroy his entire immune system in the process.
3. Inject his own stem cells back in.
4. Pray his body rebuilt itself correctly.

Simple, right?

Except it meant that before he could even get the transplant, he had to go through even more chemo.

And this time, the side effects were brutal.

✓ His skin turned gray.
✓ His lips cracked and bled.
✓ His body was literally shutting down.

And the worst part? He had no choice but to sit there and take it. This was the only way to give him a chance at survival. But as the days passed, I wondered — at what cost?

Two Months in the Hospital: The Longest Stretch Yet

After the chemo was finished, he was officially left with no immune system.

This meant:

✓ Every visitor had to be completely sanitized.
✓ Every food item had to be pre-approved.
✓ Every single germ could kill him.

For two months, he was basically a bubble boy.

And me?

I was his full-time caretaker.

✓ Going to the hospital every day.
✓ Bringing him food he could tolerate.
✓ Dealing with doctors, nurses, and endless test results.

But here's the thing about spending two straight months in a hospital as a caregiver.

It breaks you down.

My Breaking Point

I had held it together for years.

✓ Through his stubbornness.
✓ Through the first round of chemo.
✓ Through his absolute refusal to listen to doctors.

But something about this hospital stay was different.

Because this time, I was so empty. I wasn't just exhausted—I was depleted. I wasn't just frustrated—I was furious. I wasn't just worried—I was numb.

The Day I Almost Walked Away

It was a normal hospital visit. I brought him food. I made sure he had everything he needed. I sat with him while he rested.

But the entire time?

I just kept thinking…

"I can't do this anymore."

I looked at the man in the hospital bed —

The man I had spent years sacrificing everything for.

And I asked myself:

"Do I even want this life anymore?"

Because the truth was...?

Our relationship had been hanging by a thread long before cancer showed up. The emotional damage was already there. The resentment had already built up. The love I once felt had turned into obligation.

And I realized — I wasn't staying because I wanted to.

I was staying because he was a sickly man that depended on me for everything. What kind of person would that make me if I had ended things with him while he was sick? Part of it was my own conscious; the other part was worrying about the judgment I would face from others over making a decision like this while he was sick. So I stayed with him. I remember thinking at the time, once he's healthy, we can part ways.

Chapter Ten: Life After the Transplant

The transplant was done.

His immune system was rebuilding.

And now?

Now I was supposed to feel relief.

✓ Relief that the hardest part was over.
✓ Relief that he was getting stronger.
✓ Relief that maybe, finally, life could go back to normal.

But instead?

I felt nothing.

Because the truth was—

I didn't even know what *normal* looked like anymore.

After two months in the hospital, he was finally cleared to go home.

But home wasn't the same.

✓ He looked different. (Thin. Weak. Unrecognizable.)
✓ He acted different. (Quieter. More withdrawn. Less stubborn—at least for now.)

✓ Even the cats were confused. (They literally hissed at him like he was an intruder.)

But the biggest difference wasn't him.

It was me.

Because for the first time in years—

I wasn't fighting anymore.

✓ I wasn't dragging him to appointments.
✓ I wasn't arguing with doctors or insurance companies.
✓ I wasn't bribing him to do the right thing.

The war was over.

And I should have been happy.

But all I could think was:

"Now what?"

The Slow Burn of Resentment

People always assume that once a cancer patient is in remission, life just goes back to the way it was.

But they don't talk about the damage left behind.

✓ The emotional exhaustion.
✓ The resentment.
✓ The realization that everything had changed.

I had spent years sacrificing myself for him.

✓ My time.
✓ My energy.
✓ My happiness.

And now, when it was all said and done—

I didn't even know who I was anymore. Imagine that, at 36 years old, I truly didn't have a clue as to who I was. Professionally I knew my identity. Personally, I was clueless. I felt like a person just going through motions, with absolutely no feelings, completely numb.

I didn't know if I even wanted this relationship anymore.

Trying to Make It Work

I told myself, "*It's just the stress. Things will get better.*"

So I tried. I tried to reconnect with him. I tried to find joy in our relationship again. I tried to convince myself that I still wanted this. But deep down, I knew. I knew that something had shifted. And once that kind of shift happens? It's almost impossible to go back.

Chapter Eleven: The Beginning of the End

The cancer was gone. Fred had been evicted.

And yet—

I still felt like I was trapped. Because even though the medical battle was over, the emotional battle had just begun.

The Unspoken Truth

The truth was, I had been questioning our relationship long before the cancer showed up.

✓ The resentment.
✓ The exhaustion.
✓ The feeling that something just wasn't right.

I had buried it all under the weight of caregiving. Because when you're taking care of someone who's literally fighting for their life? You don't have time to sit around wondering if you're *happy*.

But now that the chaos had quieted down, the doubts were louder than ever.

The Elephant in the Room

There was no big fight.

No dramatic breakup conversation.

Just silence.

We didn't talk like we used to. We didn't laugh like we used to. We barely felt like a couple anymore.

And the worst part?

Neither of us wanted to admit it.

Guilt vs. Reality

Every time I thought about ending things, I heard the same voice in my head.

"How can you walk away now?"

"He survived cancer. You can't just abandon him."

"What kind of person would that make you?"

And so, I stayed.

Because I had spent so long taking care of him…

I had forgotten how to take care of myself.

Chapter Twelve: The Last Battle (Now with Dark Humor, Because What Else Can You Do?)

It was a Sunday.

A regular, boring, uneventful Sunday.

Or at least, it was supposed to be.

I woke up that morning, and like always, I asked my fiancé, *"What do you want for dinner?"*

He thought about it for a second and then said, *"Lasagna."*

I blinked.

Lasagna?

The man who had spent the last few months gagging at the thought of food, who had insisted everything tasted like metal or cardboard, was suddenly craving a full, multi-layered, cheese-packed, homemade Italian feast? I mean, the huge amount of chemo he had gone through totally damaged his taste buds, and here he is requesting lasagna?

Sure. Totally normal.

But hey, if my cancer survivor fiancé wanted lasagna, I was going to make him the best damn lasagna ever.

The Last Normal Moment (Or So I Thought)

I went to the store, bought everything I needed, and got to work.

✔ I chopped the onions.
✔ I browned the meat.
✔ I layered the pasta, cheese, and sauce — carefully, perfectly.

I had visions of us sitting down together, eating a nice meal, maybe even laughing for the first time in forever. I was feeling hopeful. And as I put the dish in the oven to bake, I smiled. Because for the first time in so long, things felt... normal.

Which, looking back, should have been my first red flag.

Because in my life? Anytime things start to feel "normal" — disaster is right around the corner.

The Horror Movie Scene No One Warned Me About

As the lasagna baked, I heard water running upstairs, which was weird. I peeked into the living room — he wasn't there. Then I looked down.

And that's when I saw it.

A trail of blood.

Bright red, smeared across the white tile floor.

"That's... not good," I thought to myself, in what was possibly the understatement of the year.

I ran upstairs and found him in the bathroom.

He was in the bathtub, water running—

And blood was pouring out of the hole in his chest.

It was everywhere.

All over him.

All over the tub.

And in my brain, the ER nurse version of myself was calmly assessing the situation.

✓ *Okay, this is an emergency.*
✓ *We need an ambulance.*
✓ *Apply pressure, stop the bleeding.*

But the normal, human version of me just stood there like a total idiot, thinking:

"Welp. Guess we're not having lasagna."

The 911 Call & The Moment I Became a Suspect

I grabbed the phone and dialed 911.

Operator: *What's your emergency?*

Me: *Uh, my fiancé has cancer, there's a hole in his chest, and he's currently bleeding out in my bathtub.*

Operator: *Can you be more specific?*

Me: *HE'S BLEEDING. A LOT. SEND SOMEONE NOW.*

They dispatched an ambulance.

And then, just to make things even more stressful —

The police showed up first.

And that's when another realization hit me.

"Oh my God. They're going to think I did this."

Because when I tell you my house looked like a crime scene — I am not exaggerating.

✔ Blood smeared on the floor.
✔ Blood on the stairs.
✔ Blood in the bathroom.

The moment the cops stepped inside; I could see their hands move toward their holsters.

Oh, fantastic.

They looked at me.

Then they looked at the blood.

Then back at me.

And one of them actually asked:

"Ma'am, did you do this?"

I thrust my fiancé's prescription bottles at them — the ones with "oncology" stamped on the label.

"PLEASE, HE HAS CANCER, HELP HIM."

The first officer ran upstairs.

The second officer stayed with me.

And then, through the absolute chaos, I heard the officer interrogating my half-conscious fiancé.

"Sir, did she hurt you?"

And through all of his pain, his blood loss, his slipping in and out of consciousness...

He managed to respond.

"No. She didn't. I have cancer."

And I have never been so relieved and so annoyed at the same time.

The Race to the Hospital & the Final Goodbye

They loaded him onto a stretcher.

I grabbed my car keys, ready to follow the ambulance.

But then —

"Where are they taking him?"

Not our local hospital. The trauma hospital. Thirty minutes away. Because this? This was beyond what the local ER could handle.

Despite the cancer being gone, the tumor itself refused to leave the party.

We met with multiple surgeons, even had a virtual consult with specialists in England, hoping for a miracle solution.

No luck.

The hole in his chest couldn't be repaired until the tumor was gone. The tumor couldn't be removed because it was fused to his lung and heart. The only option? Wait and hope his body would eventually break it down and absorb it.

In the meantime?

The hole had to be covered with a dressing and changed daily — a task that felt like defusing a bomb, except the bomb was his chest.

Even in a sterile environment, the risk of infection was sky-high.

It wasn't a matter of *if* an infection would happen, it was a matter of *when*. By the time I got to the hospital, the trauma team was already working on him. I sat in the waiting room, heart pounding, bracing for the worst.

And then the doctors came out.

And when there's bad news, doctors never come alone. They travel in packs, usher you into a small room, and close the door.

The Decision No One Wants to Make

For three days, they kept him on life support, pumping his body full of antibiotics for the sepsis infection. Yes, sepsis had set in.

For three days, I waited for a miracle.

But on the morning of the fourth day, the doctor pulled me aside.

"His organs are shutting down."

"There's nothing more we can do."

"It's time to say goodbye."

When the doctors told me it was time — time to turn off the machines, time to let him go — I froze.

I had spent years fighting alongside him, dragging him to chemo appointments he didn't want to go to, cleaning up after the messes that cancer (and his stubbornness) created, and pushing him to keep going, even when he didn't want to.

Now?

There was nothing left to fight for.

Just a decision.

And it was mine to make.

Why I Couldn't Stay

People always say, *"You'll regret it if you're not there when they pass."*

Maybe.

But here's the truth. I had already watched him suffer enough. I had already witnessed more trauma than I ever thought possible. I had already seen every stage of his body fighting, failing, and breaking down. I had seen him at his strongest and at his absolute weakest. I had held his hand through every part of this journey. I just couldn't watch it end.

Not Strong Enough? Or Just Human?

The guilt crept in immediately.

✔ *What if I should have stayed?*
✔ *Would he have wanted me there?*
✔ *Did I fail him in his final moments?*

But the rational side of me knew I had done everything I could for him. I had been his advocate, his support system, his caregiver. I had fought harder for his life than he ever did.

This one moment?

It didn't erase all of that.

He Was Already Gone

The reality was, he had left long before the machines turned off.

His body was just catching up.

So, when the doctors asked me if I wanted to be there, I made the hardest decision of all:

I said no.

Not because I didn't love him.

Not because I didn't care.

But because, after everything we had been through, I knew that watching him take his final breath would break me in a way I might never come back from.

I had done enough.

I had given enough.

And in that moment, I finally let myself walk away.

Chapter Thirteen: Now What?

For years, my life had been built around surviving.

✔ Surviving caregiving.
✔ Surviving medical crises.
✔ Surviving hospital visits, chemo appointments, and emergency 911 calls.

And now?

It was silent.

No doctors.
No hospitals.
No racing to the pharmacy at 11 p.m.

Just… me.

Sitting in my house.

Alone.

Surrounded by my cats, who even understood to just sit with me, and not demand food or attention.

Staring at a lasagna I never got to serve.

The Weirdness of Grief

Here's what no one tells you about grief:

It's not just crying and sadness.

It's also awkward. Like when you automatically reach for the phone to call them… and then remember they're gone. Or when people ask you how you're doing, and you honestly have no idea how to answer. Or when you realize you've spent so long taking care of someone else… you have no idea how to take care of yourself.

I wasn't just grieving him.

I was grieving the person I had been.

Because without the caregiving, the constant stress, the need to always be on high alert—

Who the hell was I? I was 37 years old, and still clueless as to who I was.

What Do You Even Do After This?

I spent the first few weeks in limbo. I went through the motions. I handled the funeral arrangements. I accepted the awkward condolences. And I was left standing there thinking, "*Okay… now what?*" I had no plan. No direction. No purpose. And as I was just beginning to process it all, life had other plans. Because while my caregiving duties for him were over… I was far from done.

Chapter Fourteen: Back to Caregiving (And Somehow, Dating?)

Just as I started processing my fiancé's passing, life had other plans.

Because caregiving?

It wasn't done with me yet.

Grief on a Schedule

I barely had time to breathe before I was back in caretaker mode. My grandmother was now in a nursing home. Although she entered the nursing home mentally sound, she developed a urinary tract infection (UTI) which went undetected for weeks. It wasn't until her mental decline and erratic behavior tipped off the staff something was wrong. She was treated with IV penicillin, and the hope was that her mind would return to normal after the 14-day treatment was completed. Unfortunately, that never happened. We were now able to add dementia to the list of ailments.

My mother was still visiting her regularly. And I was still helping where I could.

But my grandmother was declining.

And one day, we got the call.

She was gone.

Losing My Grandmother

She passed peacefully in her sleep — something I wished for every person I ever cared for. It was a blessing, and a relief.

Because even though she had physically been here, her mind had left a long time ago.

Her dementia had taken everything. She no longer recognized me. She was convinced I was out to get her. She lived in a world of paranoia and fear.

The woman who had once adored me — her only granddaughter — now saw me as a threat. I never took it personally. I knew it wasn't her. It was the disease.

But watching her disappear piece by piece was one of the hardest things I had ever experienced.

So when she finally passed? She was finally at peace.

But my mother?

She wasn't.

My Mother's Decline

My mother had never truly come to terms with my grandmother's dementia.

She had never gotten the chance to say the things she wanted to say.

And now?

She never would.

Losing my grandmother hit her hard. She was grieving. She was exhausted. And soon, her own health started to decline.

And just when I thought I'd have a break from caregiving—

I was thrown right back in.

Wait... Dating?!

Somewhere in the chaos of grief and caregiving, I had decided—

"You know what sounds like a great idea right now? Dating."

Because apparently, I was a masochist.

So I dipped my toe back into the dating world. Here I was, re-entering the dating world at 38 years old.

It was a disaster. Weird conversations. A parade of men, who couldn't pass a simple background check, made me seriously reconsider staying single forever.

And then—

I met him.

Meeting My Future Husband

So how does a middle aged woman meet her future husband? Social media of course! Now get your minds out of the gutter, we did not meet on "Tinder" – I don't even think the site existed at that point. We actually met on Facebook, through an online game played through the social media app, called "Farmville."

The Universe stepped in and decided that our paths needed to cross. The purpose of the game was to grow crops, harvest them and sell them. But you had a time limit to do so. If you waited too long to harvest your crops, they would die. If you weren't quick enough in watering your crops, they would die. To earn extra points in the game, you could help out another farm in need of a little TLC. So, that's what I did, I clicked "help another farm," and the universe brought me to his farm.

At this point, I didn't know him, and he didn't know me. But several times a week I found myself having to water his tomatoes and harvest his wheat to help him out. We only were known by our usernames in the game. And then it happened. "Farmville" neighbors merged with

"Facebook" friends, and we were now friends on Facebook.

I didn't post much on Facebook back in the day, but when I did it was funny cat memes or holiday greetings. I was more active on "Twitter" or "X" as it is known as today. I had been chatting with a nice gentleman for several weeks, we had exchanged pictures, and he finally asked me out. I accepted, and then he made the mistake so many men on social media sites do, he asked for a topless photo of me.

I sat there shaking my head with disgust and I posted my frustrations on a Facebook post. As I was drowning my sorrows in a large hazelnut iced coffee and chocolate chip muffin, I got a private message alert on Facebook. I opened it, and it was from my "Farmville" neighbor. "Scott," had taken time out of his day to send me a message, basically apologizing for all men's rude behavior, and he hoped I didn't let it ruin my day. I remember sitting there feeling stunned, hopeful, and for the first time in a very long time... happy.

Scott and I messaged each other back and forth for weeks, and finally exchanged telephone numbers. What was ironic – we lived less than 10 minutes from each other. Talk about the Universe working it's magic. In true strong woman fashion, I asked him out on a date.

It was New Year's Day, one year after my fiancé had passed away. We met at local chain restaurant for lunch. We sat down, ordered our food, started talking—and then, six hours later, the waitress came over and asked...

"Would you guys like to order dinner?"

SIX. HOURS.

We had been talking nonstop.

And that's when I knew. This man? He was different. He was kind. He was easy to talk to. He PASSED the background check!

And most important— he felt like home.

The Balancing Act: Love, Loss, and a Whole Lot of Chaos

Falling in love again while still deep in the trenches of caregiving felt… impossible. How was I supposed to open my heart to someone new— when part of it was still stuck in the past? I was dealing with my mother's health issues. I was still grieving my fiancé. And now, I was trying to navigate a new relationship.

It was like juggling flaming swords while riding a unicycle—blindfolded. It was a lot.

Loving Someone While Mourning Someone Else

Dating is hard under normal circumstances.

77

Dating while being a caregiver to my mother, which included lots of medical appointments, while still trying to figure out how to love someone new without feeling like I was betraying the past, that is next level hard. There were moments I felt guilty for moving forward.

Moments where I'd catch myself comparing—not because I wanted to, but because my brain wasn't used to the idea of someone else being in this role.

I was emotionally exhausted and constantly overwhelmed.

But somehow… he stayed.

The Patience of a Saint (Or, Why He Deserves a Trophy)

He never rushed me. He never got frustrated when I needed space. He understood that I was still figuring out how to be a person again—not just a caregiver, not just someone grieving, but me. And for the first time in a long time—I wasn't doing it alone.

Chapter Fifteen: My Mother's Battle (Or, When Life Decided to Keep Kicking Me)

If there was one thing my mother excelled at, it was keeping me on my toes. Just when I thought life might slow down, she looked at the universe and said, *"Hold my drink."*

And, unfortunately, I mean that literally.

The Existing Conditions (A.K.A. The Pre-Game Show)

Before we even get into the big diagnosis, let's review her already impressive collection of illnesses:

✔ COPD – Decades of smoking finally caught up with her lungs.
✔ Stage 2 Congestive Heart Failure – Because why have one serious condition when you can have two?
✔ And now, a return to drinking.

Yes. After 40 years of sobriety, my mother had apparently decided—

"You know what goes great with COPD? Scotch."

I didn't know about the drinking right away. I found out the fun way — by stumbling upon her hidden stash of liquor.

One day, while packing an overnight bag for one of her many hospital stays, I opened a cabinet looking for Ziplock bags... and instead, I found a half-empty bottle of Scotch.

I stood there, blinking at it, thinking, "*Huh. That's... not a Ziplock bag.*"

I proceeded to open the rest of the kitchen cabinets, looking for the Ziplock bags and all I ended up finding was what can only be described as an empty liquor bottle graveyard. There were around eight large empty Scotch bottles neatly stacked and lined up, looking like little soldiers.

It was like a morbid treasure hunt, except the prize was realizing your mother had relapsed. I stood there in shock. My mother never said anything to me about her taking up drinking again. I wasn't sure what to do, so I just closed the cabinet doors, eventually located the Ziplock bags, packed her stuff, and headed to the hospital.

On the way to the hospital, my mood was somber. I didn't want to confront her about the drinking. I figured if she had wanted me to know, she would've told me about it. So I tucked that little discovery into the vault in my brain and carried on as if nothing was wrong.

The Cancer Diagnosis (Because Life Wasn't Done Yet)

Somewhere in the middle of juggling her COPD, her heart failure, and her secret drinking habit, she started bleeding.

And not just a little.

A lot.

Now, my mother had an impressive talent for dismissing major health issues.

When the bleeding started, she shrugged and said, *"It's probably just a small cyst."*

Mind you, she was in her 80s.

There was no reason for her to be bleeding from there.

But did she rush to the doctor?

Nope.

She just casually ignored it.

Because when you've survived a two pack-a-day smoking habit and raised a stubborn daughter, what's a little unexplained hemorrhaging?

Doctor: "You Have Cancer." Mom: "Meh."

Eventually, she went to the doctor. And after several invasive tests, they finally had an answer: uterine cancer.

Her response?

"Oh."

No dramatic reaction. No panic.

Just "Oh."

Like the doctor had just informed her that it *might rain later.*

The Non-Existent Treatment Plan

Normally, when someone is diagnosed with cancer, you hear things like:

✓ *"We'll schedule surgery."*
✓ *"We'll start chemo next week."*
✓ *"Let's hit this thing aggressively."*

But not my mom. Because of her COPD and congestive heart failure, she wasn't a candidate for surgery. She also wasn't a candidate for chemo. Or radiation.

So, essentially, the doctors handed us the worst "Choose Your Own Adventure" book ever and said,

"We're just going to… see how long she lasts."

Great.

Love that for us.

Living with a Walking Time Bomb

So now we were in limbo. There was no treatment plan. There was no timeline. There were no answers.

And every few weeks, my mother would ask me—

"Is this my last spring?"
"Will I make it to Christmas?"
"Do you think I'll see another summer?"

And I would just stare at her, blinking, thinking,

"Lady, I can barely predict what I'm having for dinner, let alone how long you're going to live."

But instead, I would just sigh and say, *"I don't know, Mom."*

Because what else could I say?

Chapter Sixteen: The Final Battle (Or, When I Officially Deserved a Medal)

At this point in my life, at age 47, I had more experience with end-of-life care than most medical professionals. I had watched my father decline. I had battled "Fred" with my fiancé.
I had seen my grandmother's mind disappear into dementia.

And now?

It was Mom's turn.

Because, apparently, I was destined to be the universe's personal hospice nurse.

The Walking Medical Mystery

Despite everything going on in her body—the COPD, the congestive heart failure, the untreated uterine cancer - my mother somehow kept going.

The doctors meant well, but they couldn't answer the only question we had… how much time she had left.

One of her specialists even said, *"Your mother's body just refuses to quit."*

Which, honestly, made sense. Because if anyone could argue with death and win, it was my mother.

84

Bleeding, But Make It Fashion

One of the biggest challenges that plagued my mother was the constant bleeding. It was severe. I mean, we're talking daily crime scene clean-up levels of blood. And since she refused to acknowledge just how bad it was, my new daily routine became:

✓ Grocery shopping.
✓ Mopping up blood like I was on an episode of *CSI*.
✓ Pretending this was all totally normal.

And let's not forget the laundry. Because when someone is constantly hemorrhaging, it means relentless wardrobe changes.

I became an expert stain remover, scrubbing out blood like a seasoned forensic cleaner. They say not all heroes wear capes.

Well, I wasn't wearing a cape either, I was wearing rubber gloves and holding a mop.

Hospice, The Only Option

Eventually, it became too much. She was too weak to walk. Her breathing was getting worse. She was losing too much blood every day.

I had no choice but to call in hospice.

85

But of course, nothing about this was going to be simple.

Mom vs. Reality

I had two options for hospice care for my mother. Home hospice, where she would remain in her home, or a hospice facility. After having several conversations with the hospice team, as well as a visit to my mother while she was in the hospital receiving blood transfusions, it was determined that for her to remain at home with hospice coming in she would require a lot of care. Specifically, she was going to require a full-time live-in nurse, as well as two home health aides to assist the nurse.

Here's the thing, hospice suggested that I move in with my mother to help take care of her. Throughout my caregiving journey, boundaries were never something I set for myself. I never said "no" to any request my family made from me. This was the first and only boundary I set. And boy, did people have opinions about it.

"Shame on you for not taking care of her."

"I couldn't imagine putting my mother in a facility."

The thing was, I had a full-time job and worked from home. My job didn't start out as a work from home, but COVID took care of that. After the pandemic, my company decided to stay remote. Throughout all the stresses of being a caregiver, my only saving grace was my job. It was the one thing I could count on, the one thing that I had total control over. I had no control over the diseases that plagued my mother, or any of my family members. My job became my safe space. It helped keep my sanity, even though I was left with very little of it towards the end.

So I made the decision to put my mother in a facility. And I lucked out with the one that took her. It was closer to my house than my mother's home. The best part was there were only 10 patients. Yes, my mother was 1 of only 10 patients in the entire facility.

The facility was beautiful. The doctors, nurses, aides, and volunteers were truly incredible. The minute my husband and I walked into the facility, I was overcome with such a feeling of peace. I knew they were going to take the best care of my mother. I also remember crying because the reality hit me that this was going to be the last stop for her; this building was going to be where she would take her last breath.

My mother was transferred to the facility around 8 p.m. When the ambulance doors opened, my husband and I were there to greet her. She was happy to see us and promptly told the paramedics she had to "pee." She was laughing and seemed in good spirits.

After she went to the bathroom, the hospice team of two nurses came in and introduced themselves. They sat down with her and explained:

"You'll have round-the-clock care. You'll be comfortable. We'll manage your pain."

And my mother, in true Mom fashion, looked them dead in the eye and asked:

"So, when do I start getting better?"

The hospice nurses and I just stared at each other.

I coughed. The nurse smiled politely.

"Um... well, hospice isn't really about getting better..."

Mom frowned.

"Then why the hell are you here?"

Cue me, rubbing my temples.

This woman.

She fully understood what hospice was — she just refused to accept it.

The $11,000-a-Month Secret

As the dust settled on that first night in the hospice facility, the next nightmare became a reality. How was she going to pay for it. Medicare covers hospice care. But — surprise! — it does NOT cover room and board.

And that little detail? Cost $11,000 a month.

Excuse me, I just choked on my own oxygen.

I couldn't tell her that. She would have been horrified to know I was draining my own savings to keep her there.

So, whenever she asked, *"Who's paying for all this?"* I smiled and said, *"Medicare, Mom."* Which wasn't a total lie. It was just a carefully edited version of the truth.

Settling Into Hospice (Sort Of)

Once she was in the facility, things actually improved. She had full-time medical staff. She wasn't in pain. She got to flirt shamelessly with her male nurses. And because she wasn't home anymore, I actually had time to just be her daughter instead of her caregiver.

For the first time in years, I got to enjoy her again. And despite the incredible worry and stress I had over the cost of her care, I enjoyed all of my visits with her, all of my telephone conversations with her, all of it became cherished and precious memories.

But I also knew...

This was the beginning of the end.

Chapter Seventeen: The Last Days (Or, When My Mother Started Hanging Out with Ghosts)

There's something strange that happens when someone is nearing the end. Hospice nurses call it "visions." Science calls it "the brain's way of making sense of death."

I call it "My mother's VIP ticket to the Afterlife Social Club."

Because let me tell you — she had visitors.

Ghosts, Party of One

One day, I walked into her hospice room, and she was having a full-blown conversation… with no one.

She looked over at me, completely serious, and said:

"Oh, good! You're here! Your father and I were just talking about you!"

I smiled and went right along with it.

"Oh yeah? What were you guys saying?"

And without missing a beat, she launched into the full conversation she had apparently been having with my very-dead father. It was comforting, in a way. She wasn't afraid. She wasn't panicked.

She wasn't hallucinating like this all the time; she had very lucid moments. The hallucinations brought her so much comfort. I remember speaking with the nurses, telling them about her conversations with the "dearly departed," and explaining to them how I just went along with what she was saying and did not try to correct her. They assured me I was doing the right thing, there was no reason to upset her.

Many times, when we would chat on the phone, which was several times a day at this point, she would tell me about the two cats living in her room. She commented one day that the litter box smelled so I told her to tell the aide to clean it out. While I'm on the phone with her, she buzzes for the aide, I heard her ask the aide to clean out the litter box in the bathroom and the aide didn't miss a beat, she went into the bathroom for a bit, made some noise and told her it was all clean. I was so grateful for that.

The Rally (A.K.A. False Hope is a Jerk)

About a week before she passed, she had a burst of energy.

This is something called "The Rally."

It happens when a dying person suddenly seems like their old self again.

And let me tell you — my mother rallied HARD. She was sitting up. She was cracking jokes. She ate an entire breakfast.

The hospice nurse smiled at me and said, *"It's good to see her like this."*

And for exactly 24 hours, I let myself believe…

"Maybe she's not dying after all?"

Maybe she'll beat the odds!

Maybe she's got another year in her!

Then the next morning came.

And she was unconscious.

I swear, hope is the meanest emotion of them all.

Friday Night, The Last Visit

I sat with her for hours.

Holding her hand.

Talking to her.

She wasn't awake, but she knew I was there.

At one point, I stood up to stretch — my legs were very stiff and my butt had fallen asleep. As I stood up, the chair I was sitting in creaked a bit. And she moaned. Like she knew I was moving away. So I sat right back down.

And I told her everything.

✓ That I loved her.
✓ That I would be okay.
✓ That she didn't have to fight anymore.

And then I left.

Because part of me knew…

That was the last time I'd see her alive.

Saturday Morning, 6:35 a.m.

My phone rang. I was already awake; I had just finished feeding the cats their breakfast. It was hospice, telling me my mother had expired. Expired. Such a strange word to use to tell you that your loved one has passed away. I woke up my now husband, and we got dressed and headed to the facility to bring home her belongings.

When I got to the facility, both nurses that my mother had gotten close with over the four months she was there were both on duty. I was big and brave until I saw the sorrow in their eyes. I asked for a large garbage bag so I could gather up her clothes, and I entered her room.

Walking into the room, seeing my mother in the bed, was hard. I was nervous, afraid, sad. I had never seen a recently deceased body before. I briefly saw my father after he passed away in the ER, but he was hooked up to machines and had a mask on his face so all he looked like to me was he was sleeping. I didn't see my grandmother until the funeral, same for my fiancé. But here I was, in the room with my mother's body. I took a deep breath and walked toward the bed.

The nurses had wrapped the blankets around her so nicely, she looked like a burrito. Her facial expression was relaxed, and her eyes… were open. Despite what people see on TV, when you die, your eyes are open. Your eyes are closed while you sleep because muscles do that; when you are dead, the muscles relax and boom, open eyes.

I gathered her belongings up as quickly as I could, but I couldn't stop staring at her. I took a seat in the chair I had been in less than 12 hours prior and really looked at her. Her strength to live was so great. After about 15 minutes, I got up, creaky chair and all, and told her I would see her later at the funeral home.

As I was leaving, the nurse that called me to tell me she had passed apologized for calling me so early in the morning. I told him it was fine, I was a morning person. Actually, both my mother and I were morning people, and I would always call my mother around 6:30 a.m. every day. It was a routine we had for 20 years. 6:30 a.m. was our time. My mother took her last breath at 6:30 a.m.

Chapter Eighteen: Saying Goodbye (And Selling My Childhood in the Process)

You'd think that after experiencing so much loss, I would be a pro at handling grief.

Nope.

Turns out, grief doesn't take practice. It just wrecks you in new and creative ways each time. Losing my mother was the hardest one yet. Because she wasn't just my mom, she was my best friend.

The Funeral: One Last Show

My mother never wanted a big, dramatic funeral. No long speeches, no hysterics, no over-the-top displays of sorrow. She wanted something simple.

So we did exactly that. A quiet, respectful service. Family and close friends gathered. People sharing memories that made us laugh more than cry.

Because that's who she was.

✓ Strong.
✓ Independent.
✓ Funny as hell.

95

And if she could have attended her own funeral, I know she would have stood up, rolled her eyes, and said:

"Alright, that's enough. Someone pour me a drink."

Selling My Childhood Home: Saying Goodbye to More Than Just a Place

After the funeral, the real work began. Because now I had to do something that felt just as overwhelming as caregiving—I had to clear out and sell my mother's apartment.

Not Just a Home—A Time Capsule

This wasn't just any apartment.

This was the place where I:

✔ Had my first sleepover. Where my best friend and I giggled until 2 a.m., stuffing our faces with junk food.
✔ Played my clarinet for hours. Where my dad sat patiently, listening, even when my practicing sounded more like a dying goose than music.
✔ Watched my father slowly decline. Where every corner held a memory of him getting weaker, of my mother worrying, of me pretending everything was fine.
✔ Took care of my mother in her final years. Where I scrubbed floors, changed sheets, and made grocery runs, knowing that one day, this would all be over.

It was more than just walls and a roof.

It was a lifetime of memories.

And now?

I had to pack up an entire life into boxes and decide what stayed and what went.

The Emotional Landmine of Cleaning Out a Parent's Home

Nobody tells you how hard it is to go through a loved one's things. The clothes still hanging in the closet. The handwritten notes tucked into old books. The coffee mug they used every morning, still sitting in the cabinet. All remnants of someone's life.

Every drawer I opened felt like opening a wound.

Every decision felt too final.

✔ *Do I keep this?*
✔ *Donate it?*
✔ *Throw it away?*

And the worst part?

✔ The silence.

No more TV humming in the background.
No more sounds from the radio—my mother was a huge

fan of talk radio.
No more sounds of life.

Just me and the echoes of the past.

Letting Go—Because Holding On Wasn't an Option

Financially? I couldn't afford to keep the apartment. I had even thought of subletting it, so that I could still retain it, but I realized that for me to move on emotionally, it was time to let it go, to move forward with my life. Selling the apartment was another kind of grief.

It wasn't just losing a home.

It was losing the last tangible connection to my childhood, to my parents, to a version of my life that no longer existed.

Saying Goodbye (For Real This Time)

Selling the apartment took five months. Co-op boards are a nightmare, and selling a co-op is far more complicated than selling a house. But finally, it was done.

The paperwork was signed.

And I stood there, in that empty apartment, looking around one last time. I even took some video and pictures with my phone, so I can still "visit" the apartment when I need to.

It was sad.

But it was also time.

I had spent my entire life taking care of other people.

Now?

It was time to figure out who I was without that responsibility.

Chapter Nineteen: Life After Caregiving (Or, What Do I Do With My Hands Now?)

For thirty years, I had one identity: Caregiver.

✓ Daughter.
✓ Granddaughter.
✓ Fiancée.

It didn't matter who needed me—someone always did.

And now?

For the first time in my entire adult life...

✓ No one was calling me in the middle of the night.
✓ No one needed medications, appointments, or emergency hospital visits.
✓ No one was relying on me to keep them alive.

And I had no idea what to do with myself.

The Weirdest Kind of Freedom

There's this strange part of being a long-term caregiver that nobody talks about.

When the person you're caring for is gone...

You don't just grieve them.

You grieve your entire purpose.

✔ Who am I if I'm not taking care of someone?
✔ What do I do with all this time?
✔ Why do I feel guilty when I finally get to relax?

I had spent decades in survival mode.

Now, I was free.

And I had no idea how to handle it.

Midlife Crisis, But Make It Horse-Shaped

Several years before my mother passed away — shortly after I got married — I had my first "I need something just for me" moment.

And that moment?

Led to a horse.

✔ A big, beautiful, four-legged midlife crisis named Alfie.
✔ I named him after my father.
✔ He taught me not only how to ride, but how to be present in the moment.

Did I know anything about horses? Nope.

Did I care? Also nope.

I had spent so much time focusing on everyone else —

Now, I was going to do something just for me.

Alfie was my first step into a world that wasn't about caregiving — it was about joy.

And as the years passed, that world grew.

Because along came Copper.

And then Flame, the rescue pony.

By the time my mother passed, I already had this new, unexpected life waiting for me. A life where I wasn't just taking care of others — I was choosing what brought me happiness. A life where I could finally breathe. A life that was mine. My mother always told me she was so glad I found my passion with horses. She loved listening to my stories about them, she loved hearing about all the friends I had made, the people who I affectionately call my "barn family." She loved all of it.

From Survival Mode to Living Mode

At first, I didn't know what to do with myself.

So I started small. I let myself sleep in without checking my phone for an emergency. I let myself laugh without feeling like it was inappropriate. I let myself dream about the future without immediately thinking of someone else's needs. Little by little, I stopped just surviving.

And I actually started living.

Feeling Whole Again

Healing isn't one big moment.

It's not like you wake up one day and say, *"Yep, I'm good now!"*

It's a slow process. It's allowing yourself happiness without guilt. It's forgiving yourself for the things you couldn't change. It's learning how to live — not for others, but for yourself.

And for the first time in forever…

I felt whole.

Epilogue: A Thank You to Caregivers (Because You Deserve a Damn Medal)

Caregiving isn't something you apply for.

It doesn't come with a salary, vacation days, or an instruction manual.

You don't get to submit a resume with "Excellent at managing medical crises, hospital paperwork, and emotionally falling apart in grocery store parking lots" listed under skills.

You just do it.

Because someone you love needs you.

And so, without thinking twice, you show up.

The Job Nobody Trains You For

What people don't tell you about caregiving:

✔ You will feel exhausted, frustrated, and completely overwhelmed.
✔ You will cry privately in the car after doctor's appointments.
✔ You will lose sleep over things you can't control.

✔ You will wonder, "Am I doing enough?" (Even when you're doing everything you can and more.)

And yet, you will still keep going.

Because caregivers?

We don't quit.

Even when we're running on fumes.

Even when it feels never-ending.

Even when we have no idea how we're doing it—

We just do.

The Parts No One Talks About

You know what else they don't talk about?

✔ The anger. Yes, you love them. But that doesn't mean you won't want to scream into a pillow sometimes.
✔ The guilt. Because no matter what you do, you'll convince yourself it wasn't enough.
✔ The sheer ridiculousness of some moments. At some point, you'll find yourself cleaning up a mess, sitting in an ER at 3 a.m., or navigating yet another insurance disaster, and think, *Is this my life now?*
✔ The waiting. For test results. For the next hospital visit. For an outcome you already know is coming.

✔ The grief. Not just when they pass — but before. When you realize the person you love is slipping away long before they actually leave.

And then, there's the part they really don't prepare you for…

When It's Over, And You're Still Here

One day, the person you cared for is gone.

And for the first time in what feels like forever, there's…

✔ No phone call to return.
✔ No emergency to handle.
✔ No crisis to navigate.

The silence is deafening.

You'll feel relief, and then you'll feel guilty for feeling relief.

You'll feel lost.

Because for so long, your life was built around someone else's needs.

And now?

You have to figure out who you are without them.

To Every Caregiver Who's Been Here...

If you are still caregiving, I see you.

You are doing an impossible job, and you are doing it with more love, patience, and strength than you realize.

If you have lost the person you cared for, I see you, too.

You are still here.

You are still worthy of love, joy, and rest.

You are allowed to miss them and move forward.

You are allowed to feel both relief and sadness.

You are allowed to live for yourself now.

A Final Thought

This book is my story, but it's also yours.

To every caregiver who has ever:

✓ Held a hand through pain.
✓ Fought with doctors or insurance companies.
✓ Felt alone in the struggle.
✓ Given everything for someone they love.

This is for you.

You Want Me to Do WHAT Now? - Judith Bennett

You are seen.
You are appreciated.
And most of all — you are not alone.

Acknowledgments

Writing this book was a daunting task, and I wouldn't have been able to do it without these incredible people:

To my husband, Scott — Thank you for being my rock, my voice of reason, and the one person who never questioned my sanity (even when you probably should have). Your patience, love, and support have meant everything.

To my dear friend, Kari Marinucci — For putting up with my rants, letting me vent about the ridiculousness of caregiving, and reminding me to take care of myself (even when I ignored you).

To my inspirational friends, Sandy Trouba, Keila Jaycox & Carley Hamilton - You three were my reason for finally sitting down to write my story. The universe put us all together for a reason, and I'm so grateful.

To my horses and my cats — For being my therapy, my escape, and the best listeners I've ever had. You may not understand a word I say, but somehow, you always know when I need you most.

To every caregiver out there — This book is for you. I see you. I know how hard it is. I know how heavy the responsibility can feel. But I also know how strong you are. You are not alone.

And finally, to anyone who has ever found themselves in a situation they never signed up for and had to figure it out anyway — Welcome to the club. May we all get through it with our sanity (mostly) intact.

About the Author

Judith Bennett never planned on becoming a caregiver — it just sort of happened. For thirty years, she balanced hospitals, doctor's appointments, late-night pharmacy runs, and a steady diet of cold coffee and stress. Somewhere in between, she built a successful career as a paralegal, fell in love (twice), and discovered that humor is the only thing that keeps you sane when life refuses to slow down.

When she's not writing about the wild, messy, and unexpectedly funny side of caregiving, she can be found at the barn with her three horses, curled up with her cats, or spending time with her incredibly patient husband. She is living proof that even after decades in survival mode, it's possible to rediscover yourself — and maybe even enjoy life along the way.

This is her first book.

www.ingramcontent.com/pod-product-compliance
Lightning Source LLC
Chambersburg PA
CBHW020741130626
46554CB00006B/2099